SOUL GROWING

Wisdom for 13 year old boys from
men around the world

Collected & Edited by Quanita Roberson

SOUL GROWING

WISDOM FOR 13 YEAR OLD BOYS FROM
MEN AROUND THE WORLD

Collected & Edited by Quanita Roberson

AKAN PUBLISHING

4515 Allison Street, Suite 12412
Cincinnati, Ohio 45212-9998

Email: info@akanpublishing.com
www.akanpublishing.com

Executive Editor: Quanita Roberson

Illustration & Book Design: Elizabeth H. Murphy
www.illusionstudios.net

ISBN: 979-8-9892322-4-6 (Paperback)
ISBN: 979-8-9892322-2-2 (ebook)
Library of Congress Control Number: 2015940955

First Edition
Copyright © 2024 Quanita Roberson

Published by Akan Publishing

This book is dedicated to my two boys Jason and Jacob.
Having the pleasure of mothering you is one of the greatest joys of
my life. You have taught me more about love, patience, and loyalty
then you will ever know. I love seeing the men you are becoming. I
am so grateful and proud to know you.
This book is also dedicated to the 13 year old boys that live inside of
the men who contributed to this book.
I hope that this book is soul feeding for you.

TABLE OF CONTENTS

INTRODUCTION – ABOUT THE AUTHORS

The men who have contributed to this book are businessmen, politicians, artist, teachers, engineers, policemen, writers, and activist. They were born and raised in the United States, Canada, India, Egypt, Australia, North Korea, Brazil, Cameroon, Israel, Jamaica, and Ethiopia. They have been many things to me, my friends, brothers, cousins, teachers, students, classmates, dance partners, life partners, community children, clients, mentors, and guides. They range in age from their 20s to their 70s. They represent different religious experiences and different sexual orientations. I am in awe of their presence in the world and feel so incredibly blessed to know each and every one of them. They have crossed my path during various times in my life and have taught me more about the gifts of the masculine. Through them I have been able to strengthen my relationship to the masculine inside of me and out in the world.

BE YOURSELF

"Why fit in when you were born to stand out?"

— Dr. Seuss

RONALD V. JOHNSON

CLEVELAND, OHIO

I wish someone would have told me that I needn't work so hard to please other people. Whether it is to make new friends or find a girlfriend. I should learn to be me and those that matter will find their way to me. I spent too much time trying to make friends with people who could care less about me.

JAMES GRIFFIN

CINCINNATI, OHIO

That it's OK to be your own man and no matter what happens in life things are not as bad as they seem and there's truly nothing to fear but fear itself. I also would tell myself to not be afraid or ashamed to shine.

BOB STILGER

SPOKANE, WASHINGTON

For me, I had some amazing people in my life when I was 13, so I will answer from that context. With words and with actions they told me that I was a good person. They told me that I was making a contribution. They listened to me. Sometimes they challenged or pushed me, but mostly they just accepted me as I was. They gave me -- many older folks -- more or less unconditional support.

It is part of who I am today.

STEVEN MUNDAY

CINCINNATI, OH

Figure out who you are. Who are you?! What makes you the person you are?

Be yourself, be funny, be smart.

There ain't nothin' wrong with being smart!

MICHAEL STOLLER

OSWEGO, ILLINOIS

I wish someone would have told me when I was 13 that I was not responsible for someone else's feelings and to speak my truth.

RANDY WEEKS

DEER PARK, OH

Mostly, it comes down to being accepted just as I am, and assured that the world is likely to keep on going, and that I really can trust I'll find my way in it. . . To be told:

No matter how you feel sometimes now, the odds are actually pretty good that everything is going to be OK. Life is good and tends, mostly, to work out, so try not to worry so much.

The world at large is scary enough and your personal world is scarier, still, especially as a teen, but you can trust yourself, especially if yourself isn't too caught up in the stress and anxiety of daily modern life. So cultivate being quiet with yourself now and then, and trusting what you find in stillness, vs. in the movement of anxiety or worry.

Your experience in the world, in school and otherwise, will most often emphasize the importance of goals and of planning for success, which is a good thing. There are better goals, though. Kindness, for example, is more important than winning, more important even than wisdom.

When we're growing up we might think the best people are the strongest, or that the best people, those to be really admired and emulated, are

8

the smartest people we meet. Eventually, we discover that the very best people are the kindest people, and that those who are very kind are also strong and smart, because one has to be both smart and strong in order to be very kind. That's why, although the world has always had a whole lot of strong people and quite a few smart people, too, truly kind people have been harder to find.

Your kindness, to yourself and others, is more powerful than you may know, and it will make the world better and richer for your having been here.

RICK SCHOEFF

CINCINNATI, OHIO

To trust my own thoughts and feelings but find people with experience in things I wanted to know about, and ask them...then trust my own thoughts and feelings about what they told me - when I was 13.

MACARTHUR ANTIGUA

SHOREWOOD, WISCONSIN

I wish I had listened more to those who told me that it's OK to take a risk, and it's OK to fail. I remember at that age I was so afraid of looking dumb and foolish, that I wouldn't want to take risks - go out for a sports team, ask a classmate to the dance, etc. It took me a long time to figure out that people appreciate authentic enthusiasm more than being aloof. And more importantly, you just get to experience more if you put yourself out there and learn from failure. In addition to that, when someone says "no" to you, it's not the absolute judgment on who you are, but rather it's their opinion at that moment. And they're also subject to being wrong.

LINCOLN WARNER

SAN FRANCISCO, CALIFORNIA

Hmmm. Find "yourself", like nobody else, and BE that person. BTW, sometimes it takes a while! And to quote Dory from Finding Nemo (I have two small kids), when the water gets rough.... "just keep swimming..."

BRIAN COOVERT

PORTLAND, OREGON

I think, and this may sound simple, but I wish someone would have told me that it's important to be myself and embrace who I was when I was 13. Young people engage in so much posturing so as to seem cool or popular. I really found my happiness when I stopped trying to be someone else and just started being me.

ALISDAIR SMITH

VANCOUVER, BRITISH COLUMBIA

Learn to appreciate yourself and the gifts you bring to the world, before getting hung up on the gifts that others bring; appreciate yourself and you'll be much more able to truly appreciate others. And of course there is always Rudyard Kipling's poignant, If...

IF you can keep your head when all about you
Are losing theirs and blaming it on you,
If you can trust yourself when all men doubt you,
But make allowance for their doubting too;
If you can wait and not be tired by waiting,
Or being lied about, don't deal in lies,
Or being hated, don't give way to hating,
And yet don't look too good, nor talk too wise:

If you can dream - and not make dreams your master;
If you can think - and not make thoughts your aim;
If you can meet with Triumph and Disaster
And treat those two impostors just the same;
If you can bear to hear the truth you've spoken
Twisted by knaves to make a trap for fools,

Or watch the things you gave your life to, broken,
And stoop and build 'em up with worn-out tools:

If you can make one heap of all your winnings
And risk it on one turn of pitch-and-toss,
And lose, and start again at your beginnings
And never breathe a word about your loss;
If you can force your heart and nerve and sinew
To serve your turn long after they are gone,
And so hold on when there is nothing in you
Except the Will which says to them: 'Hold on!'

If you can talk with crowds and keep your virtue,
Or walk with Kings - nor lose the common touch,
If neither foes nor loving friends can hurt you,
If all men count with you, but none too much;
If you can fill the unforgiving minute
With sixty seconds' worth of distance run,
Yours is the Earth and everything that's in it,
And - which is more - you'll be a Man, my son!

— Rudyard Kipling

BRAD FRYE

FORT COLLINS, COLORADO

You are the most important person in the world but it is not just about you. Be confident in who you are and be sure to dream big. But be patient enough to listen to others' stories and advice: especially those with wisdom.

MODA ELGAZZAR

CINCINNATI, OHIO

My abstract advice is to live authentically and be proud of your personal history. Make lots of mistakes and don't waste them by not thinking about them. Learn from them and then make more mistakes. Don't pressure yourself to have it all figured out... Figuring it out IS the point. Be a life-long learner; cultivate your curiosity about all things. Learning and growing is hard work, but hard work can also be intense play when you do what you love. Become a master of something, do it for 10,000 hours... Then become a master of something else. You're already unique; don't pressure yourself into thinking that YOU have to express yourself all the time in order to stand out. Stand out with what you DO, not what you SAY. Take responsibility and accept your freedom. It's easier to say "sorry" early on than it is to say it when everyone is calling you out. Don't be afraid to spend time with yourself... Don't be afraid to spend time with others. Find people who will have your back and you should have their backs too. Be clear and direct... Don't beat around the bush. Say what you mean. Mean what you say. Just do you.

Most importantly, be grateful for all the experiences, learning, play, people and pain you've had throughout your life. It's what makes you you.

MARC TOGNOTTI

SAN FRANCISCO, CALIFORNIA

"Follow your own weird." That is, notice what's left behind when you catch yourself trying to act "cool" or trying to be someone you're not. Love and nourish that person — it's the real you.

DAVID HATFIELD

VANCOUVER, BRITISH COLUMBIA

I wish someone would have told me when I was 13 to totally pursue the things that I loved the most and don't doubt myself!!!

THOMAS UFER

URUÇUCA, BRAZIL

I wish someone would have told me that success is not living up to other people's expectations, it's not having a great business career or making a lot of money. It took me a lot of effort to find out that success is following your inner truth, listening to your heart and ultimately being happy! I also wish that someone would have told me that being a man is not about how strong or tough you are and how much you can endure, but about how much you can be yourself, express your true feelings, be vulnerable yet resilient, be firm yet caring, and above all about how much you can respect and protect the people you care about... what really makes you a man is ultimately your ability to express your power through love!

CHANDLER STEVENS

CINCINNATI OHIO

When I was 13, I wish more than anything that I learned how to listen to my own voice.

SCOTT KISSEL

CINCINNATI, OHIO

Tune in and trust the truths of your young self, of your childhood boy-ness. Whatever it is that lights you up, turns you on, brings you happiness, transports you to yourSELF as a young person is a clue to what you are meant to do and be and to your purpose going forward. The culture and the world may tell you that there is a good, right, best way to become successful, to live in "the real world," to live your life. But let your deepest, earliest, truest inklings and urges guide you.

As a boy, I learned how to cut, repair and install glass because even at the tender age of 5, all I wanted to do was tag along with my dad and grandpa to our family glass business. I grew up there, doing anything and every-thing, eager to prove I could do it, too. At one point, once I had become a full-fledged glazier, my dad asked me, "How did you learn to cut, hold and carry glass like that? I never taught you that." (A proud moment for me). I learned from him, yes - but I was also self-directed and self-taught. The hands-on work came readily to me. It's just something I was meant to do.

Still, many looked down on me. Expected me to do, be or seek something different, something "more." Go to college. Expand my horizons. So, for quite some time, I left glass work in pursuit of other more culturally acceptable work, trying to fit into some mold that wasn't made for me.

Don't get me wrong - college and "more" and exploration and discovery is fine. But remaining true to what you already know vs. attempting to rise to anyone else's standard is legitimate and valuable. You doing what you're ultimately put here to do is the most important thing. And the clues to what that really is don't come from test scores and class rankings, they don't come from prestigious universities or a long list of accomplishments. They definitely don't come from the expectations of your parents or others — they are imprinted within and, I wish someone had told me that it's important to tune in and follow the wisdom of my young boy self.

MICHAEL WEHLING

SEATTLE, WASHINGTON

I wish someone would have told me that I didn't need to be ashamed of who I was, how I felt, what I did to cope with the difficult circumstances around me, nor what I hoped for in my life.

REX LAI

CINCINNATI, OHIO

When I was 13, I felt like I was born with 2 tongues. As a proud Taiwanese and as a proud American, I always felt like I was hopping in and out of 2 different worlds. What I realize now is, that this hopping was really a dance I learned to become the unique person I am today. There is no one like me. That's pretty cool.

KEN NEIHEISEL

AUSTIN, TEXAS

<u>Connect</u> with your HEART

<u>Feel</u> what's inside of your HEART

<u>Follow</u> where your HEART leads you.

LIFE LONG LEARNING

Live as if you were to die tomorrow. Learn as if you were to live forever.

— Mahatma Gandhi

DAMAREO COOPER

AKRON, OHIO

I wish someone would have told me that I was valuable and important, and that many people had lived and died for the sake of my success. That I shouldn't be afraid to fail because in failure we learn our greatest lessons and that through these lessons we have our greatest victories.

MINH N. TRUONG

CINCINNATI, OHIO

Never stop learning new things.

MICHAEL O'BANION

WESTMINSTER, MARYLAND

I would like you to think of the subject of learning new things, including skills, crafts, work, games, sports, volunteer work, new subjects in school, and many others I can't think of right now. For the purpose of this discussion hopefully the new "things" you will learn, please keep them within the boundaries of moral, ethical, and legal acceptability.

When you have an opportunity to learn or experience something new, you will likely have some preconceived positive or negative ideas or feelings about the subject. One of your friends may have said, "Oh, I don't like that." Don't let yourself be swayed by these thoughts or ideas, but rather enthusiastically explore the new opportunity. Actually participate actively as much as you can. Learn everything about the subject, until you clearly know you like or do not like the subject, sport, skill, craft, etc. Adopting this attitude will do several things for you. You will know, with your own real experience, what you like and what you do not like. You will learn what you are really good at and what you may be not so good at.

This becomes really important in your life as you first consider what curriculum to take in college, or what job you may have to consider working. I know many people who went to college because they liked a course in high school, and mostly they had a very good teacher, then were really not happy with their decision. That is usually not a good indicator that you will like a college curriculum and further you may not like the work you would be doing after college utilizing the college learnings. Having the actual experience of a job can help you.

Further, these experiences will come back to you throughout your life. As you are doing something, you will have the satisfaction of knowing "I know how to do this" because of your prior experience.

NEIL ANDERSON

CINCINNATI, OHIO

Be a student of Life for Life. Cultivate the mind AND the heart. When self doubt visits, be open to what it has to show you. Be willing to take a few detours to reach your goals because everything in your experience is part of the path and it will not be a straight one. Find balance in all things. Love has no gender. It is why you are here.

NORRIS WILLIAMS

Men of age that are established, and spiritually grounded, always give good advice to make your life better.

TERRY (MERLIN) BAKER

HAWKER, AUSTRALIA

All of us are creative artists. We are on this planet to invent ourselves.

The best way to be creative and invent something is to start by asking good questions. Here are a few to get you started. They are only a start. To continue inventing and creating yourself, please continue to ask good questions. Cultivate curiosity.

What is my greatest fear, and what am I willing to do to diminish it?

How can I become smarter about the way I love?

What pose would it be a big relief to drop?

Which of my wounds is primed for a dramatic healing, and what is the best way to begin the cure?

What am I grateful for today?

Who loves me and who do I love?

What do I appreciate about my life today?

What am I happy about in my life right now?

What am I proud about in my life right now?

What did I learn today?

These questions have come from various sources, such as Richard Moss, and Anthony Robbins.

RICK SHICK

COLORADO SPRINGS, COLORADO

Study music, learn to sing and learn to make music with others.

DEONDRA KAMAU MEANS

CINCINNATI, OHIO

Learn to save. And know that what you do today prepares you for your success tomorrow.

RICK WARM

CINCINNATI, OHIO

I wish someone had told me to "learn for life" and not learn just for school and tests when I was 13. The truth is, someone did tell me that when I was about 17. He was a teacher of mine in an AP History class who clearly loved what he taught. He would always say, "study for life, not for the test." But he still was a teacher and gave us tests and grades and everyone knew that if you didn't get a good grade on the tests, you wouldn't get a good grade on your report card. It took me graduating from high school, college, and graduate school and into my young professional life, study-ing for the test, before I realized what my teacher meant (but couldn't really uphold). Studying, or rather learning is an act of love. When we learn for life, as opposed to learning for a test, we not only are better able to apply what we learn, but we develop a temperament of what can be called lifelong learning. Not only do we realize that learning helps us constantly grow and develop into the kind of person we truly can be, but it also educates us that change is the only real constant and prepares us to deal with change every day -- even when we don't want to change. Of course you will find that you will still have to learn for the test, and there will be subjects that you don't like and can't see the point of studying. But in general, if you begin to appreciate that learning is important for life and growth, you will always be that much more ahead of the curve and able to lead change and not just follow.

ELIJAH HAKIM-ADONIJAH

WINDEMERE, FLORIDA

I actually would completely repeat Rick's reply word for word. Yet at the age of 13 you are a product of your environment and the bully system among adults and society tends to help shape a 13 year old's decision to go a certain direction. I think the real lesson that needs to be learned - by parents who are or will parent a 13 year old - is to connect with their emotions and their passion even if it is something that is against the status quo of society.

JONATHAN GUINN

MANHATTAN, NEW YORK

I think a lot of people told me a lot of things when I was younger and the problem is I didn't listen. And so I just wish someone would have made me listen and follow their guidance with strong conviction. You mentioned that some guy told you to make all the mistakes you can early. And yeah, that's one way of learning, through cause and effect. But a way to learn with much less anxiety and suffering is to just listen to what people with more experience are telling you.

I wish I would have listened to my elders more. Getting older, I am start-ing to realize the value of all the things my elders were trying to get in my head. To stop wasting time doing things like watching TV and playing video games and start doing the things that you really want to do. I wish that someone would have told me that selfishness and an over consump-tion of pleasure would lead to misery. I wish I would have listened to people telling me to eat healthier and study harder and to treat people better, and to stay away from things that defile the self. Recently I began to study Buddhism and it has helped me to realize all of these things. And it has helped me to balance my life into something focused much less on the pleasures of the secular world, and to try to find my purpose from within. It has helped me to treat people better. It has made me a better son, a better brother, and a better friend, and it has instilled a great sense of peace in me. I just feel lucky that I have realized all of this now in my mid 20s and not in my mid 40s or on my death bed, like most people do. I feel delivered from ignorance, knowing that I don't have to carry on in life worrying about all of the things 90% of people in the world waste their time worrying about.

FEELINGS & EMOTIONS

Thoughts are the shadows of our feelings -
always darker, emptier and simpler.

— Friedrich Nietzsche

UKUMBWA SAUTI M.ED.

ARLINGTON, MASSACHUSETTS

"....that I was worthy of love..... "

Dream new worlds free of oppression and privilege, dream of men in balance and powerful supportive, loving communities.

MARK JEFFREY

VANCOUVER, BRITISH COLUMBIA

You are wise. You have wisdom; wisdom that can guide you. Your wisdom can help you find answers to questions; it can tell who to turn to for answers. And, most importantly, it can help find the right questions.

You can access your wisdom through stillness; by being quiet; by walking in nature. If you can turn off the phone, computer, TV, games, and every other distraction, your wisdom will show itself.

Your mind does not always like when you get in touch with that wisdom and can cause you to be anxious or scared or angry. The wisdom is calm and a place to find courage.

Your wisdom exists in you now, it will grow, and it will always be there.

RYAN KOWDLEY

SAN FRANCISCO, CALIFORNIA

I wish someone had told me that none of this was going to matter in 5 years with the exception of how you did in school. I also wish someone had told me that the secret to relationships is being the one to take the first step, and generally how important the ability to build relationships is. Treat people as well as you can, give respect and be genuine about it, and more often than not you will receive it in turn. People tend to like people who like them. It's as simple as that.

JOHNATHAN BARBER

CINCINNATI, OHIO

Life is unfair, cold, brutal, and unbalanced. There will be times when sur-
render or anger seems appropriate. A weak man will give in...get angry...
point the finger...react with emotion. A strong man will find a way to USE
THE CIRCUMSTANCE as a catalyst for positive change. A strong man
will fight to find a way to use adversity as inspiration rather than a handi-
cap. Life is going to knock you on your ass, but a real man is going to learn
from each punch and become stronger each time.

SEAN MCGOVERN

"Our job is to love others without stopping to inquire whether or not they are worthy. That is not our business and, in fact, it is nobody's business. What we are asked to do is to love, and this love itself will render both ourselves and our neighbors worthy."

— Thomas Merton

That said:

If you express yourself as a giving person, you will be easily taken advantage of. It's important to set limits, especially with those that we love the most. It's impossible to be all things to all people, and unless we set financial, time, emotional limits on what we're willing to invest in others, we slowly lose the capacity to love at all.

When you pick a battle, fight to win, not glorify yourself.

Avoid the temptation to believe that redemption is born through suffering. People that love you want you to be happy.

"I don't know" is often the wisest answer.

Men carry a tremendous amount of privilege, and with that comes responsibility. Some will resent you for your privilege and gender. Be an advocate and model for a compassionate and responsible masculine role as society figures this out.

You are a child of God and stardust. You are a unique and beautiful being with limitless potential. Don't waste the time you have with yourself.

BERTIN ONDJA'A

CINCINNATI, OHIO

My mother is a rare flower that is watered by my love and to deprive her of that love is to kill her. She is the only person that prays to leave this world before me.

KENN DAY

CINCINNATI, OHIO

Remember that you did not come into this world on your own. You would not be here without your parents. They deserve acknowledgement for this, if nothing else. We stand on the shoulders of those who come before us.

AMAHA SELLASSIE

DAYTON, OHIO

I wish someone would have told me that my wealth was in the quality not quantity of my relationships with others when I was 13. Love is power, and when I walk with genuine love for people I can do anything but fail. Forgiveness has the power to heal all relationships. Genuinely seek to be a friend and develop your heart to have love and compassion, for love can turn your enemy into your friend. Trust is the key to building and maintaining relationships. Without it we cannot cooperate with one another or do great things together. Every day, and in every relationship we have the opportunity to make stronger our fragile bridge of trust between us. Great relationships take time to build, and requires investing time to develop. It is more important to listen and understand someone rather than being understood. Assume the best in people and have patience with them, just as there are times when we want people to be patient with us and assume the best of us. We all have wants, dreams, fear, pain, embarrassment, and doubt, etc. Knowing that we have this in common enables us to know we are normal when we feel these things as well.

TIM GLEIM

VIRGINIA BEACH, VIRGINIA

Dream - never stop dreaming. Use your imagination. Treat people with kindness and respect - the way you would want to be treated. And - tell your parents you love them as often as you can (even when you are embarrassed to be seen with them in public).

PHIL MINEER

CINCINNATI, OHIO

I found that happiness came from making things simple. So I only have three goals that are long term and the rest are temporary: 1– Try to be the best person I can be, not just for others but for myself.
2 – Love as much and as deeply as possible. Life is too short to be afraid to love, but love is about appreciation not possession. 3 – I want to look back on my life when I am old and know that I made the world better than when I was born into it.

As long as everything I do is accomplishing one or more of these goals I am happy and things fall into place.

CHANDU TENNETY

COLUMBUS, OHIO

Remember that perfect doesn't mean infallible; frail doesn't mean weak; strong doesn't mean right. Start with empathy; love will follow.

DO YOUR BEST

Always Do Your Best. Your best is going to change from moment to
moment; it will be different when you are healthy as opposed to sick.
Under any circumstance, simply do your best,
and you will avoid self-judgment, self-abuse and regret.

— Miguel Angel Ruiz

ERIC HANSEN

CINCINNATI, OHIO

Don't rely on talent or natural ability. Value practice, paying attention when you practice, and finding a mentor/teacher you can trust. Get better every day. Whatever you do, do it to the best of your ability – try to go all in. If you can't go all in, take a hard look at what you are doing. Is it what you really want to do?

AHMED AMIN HOSNI

MOOSE JAW, SASKATCHEWAN

I would say that perseverance is a virtue. Setting goals and committing to getting them done is the way to success.

GREG LOWRY

CINCINNATI, OHIO

I wish someone would have told me to practice more and to take drum lessons to learn properly about my gift God has given me. I know I could have been so much better if I would have been taught the basics early. I was always told how good I was or when I was in high school band was always teaching others. I just wish someone would have told me I had so much more to learn and would have taught me. I hope that makes sense.

STEVEN WALLIS

PETALUMA, CALIFORNIA

I wish someone would have told me when I was 13 that the secret to life is learning to push myself to accomplish greater things - even when I am tired or bored.

JOE MEIROSE

SACKETS HARBOR, NEW YORK

Everyone is pretty good at doing what they like to do. The key to success is doing good at the things they don't like as well.

LUCAS ALBUQUERQUE

CUIABÁ, BRAZIL

When I was 13, I wish someone would have told me to go slow and to make plans, try to build things strongly, and never never give up.

WARD MAILLIARD

WATSONVILLE, CALIFORNIA

Hmmmmm.........Advice...............Listen with curiosity and some caution to advice from well meaning adults. We all have unfinished business that we hope someone will take care of. If you want to be happy (and I mean this), loving relationships and serving something greater than yourself are the keys. If you want to be successful show up, pay attention, contribute. I've probably already gone over the limit of what is useful. Don't forget to have fun!

WORK & MONEY

Human beings are much bigger than just making money.

— Muhammad Yunus

KURT BACHMAN

CINCINNATI, OHIO

Slow down and don't grow up too fast. Learn all you can about the things you love. Feed your passions and hobbies so they grow. Be very mindful in the choices you make. Learn the value of money and also recognize that it is only paper. Eat as healthy as you can, especially during your developmental stages in life.

BASETTE SMITH

CINCINNATI, OHIO

...to put $20 a month (or any amount, for that matter) in a savings account...

BRIAN GIBBEMEYER

YPSILANTI, MICHIGAN

I usually ask people who are just going into college, what kind of person do you want to be? If there is someone in their life that they admire that they should figure what they did to get there and do it. Second, if someone is doing something better than you (cooking, working, playing, etc.) and they offer advice—take it. A lot of people offer advice. The advice may sound good on paper but if they don't practice that heuristic themselves then they don't believe in what they are saying.

VERNON JACKSON

CINCINNATI, OHIO

It's better to save first. Then pay bills. Then have fun.

BEN KAUFMAN

CINCINNATI, OHIO

That I should have joined the Coast Guard reserve as soon as I was old enough . . .

I spent the years 17-33 evading the draft in ways that affected school and job choices. I didn't want to go to Korea or Vietnam. Friends who joined the USCG Reserve enjoyed the experience, never saw active duty after six months of boot camp and two week annual drills, and had VA benefits for the rest of their lives. They were draft free by the time they entered college.

STEVEN J. BAINES

CINCINNATI, OHIO

People are always paying attention to you, even when you think they aren't, so always be presentable and use good manners. You'll stand out from the crowd and be blessed with opportunities.

JUSTIN BORGMAN

ATLANTA, GA

Save more money!!

PURPOSE
& LIVING IN THE NOW

The purpose of our lives is to be happy.

— Dalai Lama

DENNY STOCKDALE

MINNEAPOLIS, MINNESOTA

I wish someone would have told me what my purpose in life was going to be.

JEFFRY POOLE

LOS ANGELES, CALIFORNIA

Enjoy and live in the NOW, but realize that it is only a very small part of the journey. And it sounds cheesy, but Dr. Seuss's first book was rejected by 27 different publishers, so believe strongly enough in yourself and others will begin to believe in you too! Oh, and play sports, any sport, even if you are not good at it. The friendships and health benefits you'll receive are worth it!

YANIV ABOTBUL

ST. PAUL, MINNESOTA

To live for today.

AKWESI PRINCE MENSA

CINCINNATI, OHIO

For me, practice more mediation for cultivating self love; write more
poetry, break dance more, and be more of a leader.

VINCENT L. BRILEY

DAVENPORT, IOWA

Keep room in your life for "Both / And". I can't tell you how much it has helped me over the years - even when I met my own father for the first time 11 years ago. "Both / And" provides an opportunity for grace in your life, which is important to learn while you're young.

BEN KEEBLER

INDIANAPOLIS, INDIANA

Find a purpose that fulfills mind body and spirit in positive ways and that serves others.

TENNESON WOOLF

LINDON, UTAH

I love this question, from the perspective of my inner 13 year old, and (from) a few other levels too.

I found myself with several bits of guidance: Some that just works for me; some that I've shared with my son; some deep, some playful. Here's my mix:

Welcome surprises.
Do things anonymously for people.
Be good to yourself.
Don't forget you have important things to do in this life.
If you do forget, I'll knock your block off! (what I tell my kids)
Everyone has stuff to deal with. This is some of yours / ours.
Create cool stuff.
I'm proud of you.
There is always another way.
Do good stuff after school.
Get a slurpee every now and then.

JUSTIN WILLIAMS

CINCINNATI, OHIO

That I was everything that God says I am.

MOOJI

Neither take life too personally nor believe everything you see or feel. Try to observe with detachment rather than identifying with your initial reactions. Learn to observe things and people without judgments or interpretation. As you continue observing with detachment you will begin to feel a lot of space opening up inside yourself and you will enjoy this. Gradually, you will come to discover that life takes care of life much more than we imagine it does. Much peace, wisdom and a natural joy will shine inside your being.

ABOUT THE AUTHORS AND THIS BOOK

In this book Quanita serves as host, bringing together men from around the world to help support boys 13 years old and older.

According to the Dagara Medicine Wheel of West Africa I am a Water Spirit. I am the promise of forgiveness and reconciliation in the world. I bring the emotions and serve as peace maker and bridge builder in the communities of which I am a part. This is my purpose. This is the medicine that I bring. The funny thing about the gifts we are born with is that we don't have to even try that hard for them to be effective. They are a part of who we are and most of the time we take them for granted because they come so easily. You have your own gifts and all you have to do to discover them is to slow down and take a look at who you have been and what comes easily for you. This simple act will give you clues.

"Writers imagine that they cull stories from the world. I'm beginning to believe that vanity makes them think so. That it's actually the other way around. Stories cull writers from the world. Stories reveal themselves to us. The public narrative, the private narrative - they colonize us. They commission us. They insist on being told. Fiction and nonfiction are only different techniques of story telling. For reasons that I don't fully understand, fiction dances out of me, and nonfiction is wrenched out by the aching, broken world I wake up to every morning." — Arundhati Roy, The God of Small Things

This book definitely found me and not the other way around. As a matter of fact I was in the middle of writing another book when a young man that I know had his 13th birthday and I wanted to acknowledge this important rite of passage in his life by sending him words of advice from men that I knew. It wasn't until later when the men started to suggest that this might be a book that I started to think of the possibility. I got the idea for this gift late one night and woke up early and sent out a message that said:

Hello all,

I know a young man who has just turned 13 and I am sending him words of wisdom from men that I know and respect (and you made the cut) for 13 days. If I get more then 13, what a blessing. I am trying to acknowledge this Rites of Passages of him becoming a teenager. If you are willing and able would you please fill in the blank for the statement below?

I wish someone would have told me _____when I was 13.
You can post it here or email it to me

Thank you for being in my life and being so wonderful that there would be no doubt to me that you would be on this list.

Much love, Q

Little did I know when I sent out this request what amazing gifts would come from it, not just for the young man but for all who participated in this project. The gifts multiplied as gifts often do. In total I ended up with 66 quotes from a diverse group of men. The men come from different counties, cultures, races, ages, sexual orientations, professions, and religions. I didn't consciously choose a diverse group but as I said above I am a peace maker and bridge builder so when I turned to my community this is what it looked like. One of the first gifts that struck me was the realization that I knew so many amazing men. It surprised and delighted me. The second gift was in reading the responses from these men who I knew, men who I have varying degrees of relationships with. Reading these heartfelt responses helped me to feel closer to them, it added to my stories with them. Their replies spoke to who they are in the world. There are bits of information that I know, because of my individual relationships with them, that adds to the depth of connection that we share. The group of men included men that have sons around the age of 13, men who have sons who are now adults, men who fathered girls, men whose fathers have died or were in the process of dying as they replied, men whose father's died when they were young and men who never knew their fathers. There were times when I could see how their experiences informed their responses and it just made them more precious to me. The third gift came about because I sent the request to the men through a message on Facebook. Because I had chosen to use this mode of communication the men were able to see each other's responses. Some of the men in private conversations with me expressed their gratitude in being asked as well as being able to see the other men's responses one even wrote:

"Thank you so much! It is an honor to be thought of in this manner. I think all of us men who received this from you thought about when we were 13 and what we knew then and what we know now. I can't speak for everyone but that 13 year old boy still lives inside. He is who keeps me interested in what more there is to learn. After reading the other post.....it made me think how there are many things I wish I had been told...I just hadn't realized it yet!"

The fourth gift was being able to bear witness to their generosity. They showed up in service to a young boy that only one of them knew and they gave of themselves in a deep and simple way.

A friend once shared with me a story that she had heard about how we have it backwards in our culture we think that the men carry the power and the women carry the love but when we are at our best it is just the opposite. The men show up from a place of love and step into service and the women hold and use their power to create and to say enough. I love what happen here without us even being aware of it. I showed up and used my power to create space for the men to use their wisdom and they filled that space with more love then I could have imagined.

So why is all of this important you might ask? Because we are in a time when there is a rise in the feminine. In 2008 Bishop Desmond Tutu describes why he believes it's time for the world to recognize women as leaders, in a discussion held at the World Affairs Council. In 2012 the Dalai Lama said that he is a feminist and that Western women will save the world. In Jean Shinoda Bolen's book, *The Millionth Circle: How to Change Ourselves and the World,* talking about women's circles she writes, "Until now, nothing was available to inspire, instruct, and capture the imaginations of the millions of women engaged in what we will eventually recognize as the social, cultural, and psychospiritual transformation of our time." In this transformation we can't afford to lose our boys, and our men have the wisdom to bring them along, but we have to create spaces for this to happen. My hope is that this book helps to create such a space.

QUANITA ROBERSON, MA

Quanita Roberson is the Founder and Director of Nzuzu (www. nzuzu.com), a personal and professional development resource dedicated to addressing embedded trauma through healing workshops, retreats, and rituals including the Global Day of Grieving for Descendants of Slaves.

As a spiritual teacher, writer, facilitator, speaker and integral life coach, Quanita inspires people to embrace self-awareness and self-acceptance. She knows the power of personal story as medicine, and she collects and shares the medicine stories of others along with her own.

Quanita has been working as a life coach for over 10 years, and holds a Master's degree in Organizational Management and Development, with a concentration in Integral Theory.

Quanita is a native and resident of Cincinnati, Ohio, and the mother of two children of the millennial generation.

Books by Dos Madres Press

Mary Margaret Alvarado - *Hey Folly* (2013)

John Anson - *Jose-Maria de Heredia's Les Trophées* (2013),
   Time Pieces - poems & translations (2014)

Jennifer Arin - *Ways We Hold* (2012)

Michael Autrey - *From The Genre Of Silence* (2008)

Stuart Bartow - *Einstein's Lawn* (2015)

Paul Bray - *Things Past and Things to Come* (2006), *Terrible Woods* (2008)

Ann Cefola - *Face Painting in the Dark* (2014)

Jon Curley - *New Shadows* (2009), *Angles of Incidents* (2012)

Grace Curtis - *The Shape of a Box* (2014)

Sara Dailey - *Earlier Lives* (2012)

Dennis Daly - *Nightwalking with Nathaniel-poems of Salem* (2014)

Richard Darabaner - *Plaint* (2012)

Deborah Diemont - *Wanderer* (2009), *Diverting Angels* (2012)

Joseph Donahue - *The Copper Scroll* (2007)

Annie Finch - *Home Birth* (2004)

Norman Finkelstein - *An Assembly* (2004), *Scribe* (2009)

Karen George - *Swim Your Way Back* (2014)

Gerry Grubbs - *Still Life* (2005), *Girls in Bright Dresses Dancing* (2010),
   The Hive-a book we read for its honey (2013)

Richard Hague - *Burst, Poems Quickly* (2004), *During The Recent Extinctions* (2012),
   Where Drunk Men Go (2015)

Ruth D. Handel - *Tugboat Warrior* (2013), *No Border is Perennial* (2015)

Pauletta Hansel - *First Person* (2007), *What I Did There* (2011), *Tangle* (2015)

Michael Heller - *A Look at the Door with the Hinges Off* (2006), *Earth and Cave* (2006)

Michael Henson - *The Tao of Longing & The Body Geographic* (2010)

R. Nemo Hill - *When Men Bow Down* (2012)

W. Nick Hill - *And We'd Understand Crows Laughing* (2012)

Eric Hoffman - *Life At Braintree* (2008), *The American Eye* (2011), *By the Hours* (2013),
    Forms of Life (2015)

Roald Hoffmann - *Something That Belongs To You* (2015)

James Hogan - *Rue St. Jacques* (2005)

Keith Holyoak - *My Minotaur* (2010), *Foreigner* (2012),
    The Gospel According to Judas (2015)

Nancy Kassell - *Text(isles)* (2013)

David M. Katz - *Claims of Home* (2011), *Stanzas on Oz* (2015)

Sherry Kearns - *Deep Kiss* (2013), *The Magnificence of Ruin* (2015)

Marjorie Deiter Keyishian - *Ashes and All* (2015)

Burt Kimmelman - *There Are Words* (2007), *The Way We Live* (2011)

Jill Kelly Koren - *The Work of the Body* (2015)

Ralph La Charity - *Farewellia a la Aralee* (2014)

Pamela L. Laskin - *Plagiarist* (2012)

Owen Lewis - *Sometimes Full of Daylight* (2013), *Best Man* (2015)

Richard Luftig - *Off The Map* (2006)

Austin MacRae - *The Organ Builder* (2012)

Mario Markus - *Chemical Poems-One For Each Element* (2013)

J. Morris - *The Musician, Approaching Sleep* (2006)

Patricia Monaghan - *Mary-A Life in Verse* (2014)

Rick Mullin - *Soutine* (2012), *Coelacanth* (2013), *Sonnets on the Voyage of the Beagle* (2014)

Fred Muratori - *A Civilization* (2014)

Robert Murphy - *Not For You Alone* (2004), *Life in the Ordovician* (2007),
     From Behind The Blind (2013)

Pam O'Brien - *The Answer To Each Is The Same* (2012)

Peter O'Leary - *A Mystical Theology of the Limbic Fissure* (2005)

Bea Opengart - *In The Land* (2011)

David A. Petreman - *Candlelight in Quintero-bilingual ed.* (2011)

Paul Pines - *Reflections in a Smoking Mirror* (2011),
     New Orleans Variations & Paris Ouroboros (2013),
     Fishing on the Pole Star (2014)
     Message from the Memoirist (2015)

Quanita Roberson - *Soul Growing-Wisdom for thirteen year old boys from men
     around the world* (2015)

William Schickel - *What A Woman* (2007)

Don Schofield - *In Lands Imagination Favors* (2014)

David Schloss - *Behind the Eyes* (2005), *Reports from Babylon and Beyond* (2015)

Daniel Shapiro - *The Red Handkerchief and other poems* (2014)

Murray Shugars - *Songs My Mother Never Taught Me* (2011), *Snakebit Kudzu* (2013)

Jason Shulman - *What does reward bring you but to bind you to Heaven like a slave? (2013)*

Maxine Silverman - *Palimpsest (2014)*

Lianne Spidel & Anne Loveland - *Pairings* (2012), *A Bird in the Hand* (2014)

Olivia Stiffler - *Otherwise, we are safe* (2013)

Carole Stone - *Hurt, the Shadow-the Josephine Hopper poems* (2013)

Nathan Swartzendruber - *Opaque Projectionist* (2009)

Jean Syed - *Sonnets* (2009)

Eileen R. Tabios - *INVENT[ST]ORY Selected Catalog Poems and New 1996-2015* (2015)

Madeline Tiger - *The Atheist's Prayer* (2010), *From the Viewing Stand* (2011)

James Tolan - *Red Walls* (2011)

Brian Volck - *Flesh Becomes Word* (2013)

Henry Weinfield - *The Tears of the Muses* (2005), *Without Mythologies* (2008),
      A Wandering Aramaean (2012)

Donald Wellman - *A North Atlantic Wall* (2010), *The Cranberry Island Series* (2012)

Sarah White - *The Unknowing Muse* (2014)

Anne Whitehouse - *The Refrain* (2012)

Martin Willetts Jr. - *Secrets No One Must Talk About* (2011)

Tyrone Williams - *Futures, Elections* (2004), *Adventures of Pi* (2011)

Kip Zegers - *The Poet of Schools* (2013)

www.dosmadres.com

www.ingramcontent.com/pod-product-compliance
Lightning Source LLC
Chambersburg PA
CBHW041145120626
46547CB00020B/3118